WAIT MEANS YES

A Guide to Wait on the Promises of God

By

Kiameshea Brown

Dedication

To Brayden, my greatest gift from God, I have learned so much being your mom. I love you more than all the Legos in all the world.

To Mr. God Sent, I am preparing my heart to give you love and receive your love in return. I pray for you regularly.

To everyone who is waiting on a promise from God...

The Lord isn't really being slow about his promise, as some people think. No, he is being patient for your sake. He does not want anyone to be destroyed but wants everyone to repent.

2 Peter 3:9 (NLT)

Acknowledgment

To my mom, Linda, who encouraged my love for God and books and for being present for the highs and the lows. Thank you for the way you love Brayden; I love you to the moon and back.

To my sisters, Toya, my biggest supporter, for always seeing the greatness in me, even when I struggle to see it, and Brea, my hype man, thank you for all the books and conversations that helped me grow. Y'all are the best gift Daddy ever gave me.

To my nieces, Jaylinn and Ly'Chelle, your unconditional love makes me feel ten feet tall. I pray that this book guides you through life. "Gimme some fin, Noggin', Dude!!"

To Aunt Val, thank you for building my self-esteem and planting the seed of the gospel in my heart.

To Rainy and Sharetta, thank you for holding me accountable in love and for walking through life with me.

To my pastors, Elder Myron and Lady Kim, thank you for encouraging the growth in God and for your support and prayers. May God answer every prayer concerning you.

Introduction

There is always that ONE thing that we REALLY want God to do for us. It's the thing that our heart desires the most. It might be healing for you or a loved one, the ability to conceive a child, a spouse to share your life with, or a career that is fulfilling. Regardless of what IT is, there is something that each of us desires and needs God's assistance and guidance in. A lot of time, we assume that if God answers THIS prayer, our lives will be full, complete, and perfect, which is rarely the case. (Topic for a different chapter). I don't know much about you, so let me talk about me. I am a single woman who was addicted to romance novels. Ask any of my family or friends and they will tell you there was ALWAYS a book in my bag. So naturally, my desire was to get married and have a family. In 2006, I broke up with my college sweetheart because it was clear we wanted different things. In 2007, I was disappointed (distraught) that he hadn't realized that he had made the biggest mistake of his life by letting me "get away" and perform an epic romantic gesture to win me back (romance novel plot working against me). So, my attitude began to shift (and not in a good and positive way.) It was during this shift that the Godly people in my life tried to talk some sense into me and encourage me. This was the first time someone told me to wait concerning this specific desire of mine. I grew up in church, so I had read (well, heard) the scripture, "They that wait on the Lord shall renew their strength…" blah blah blah. While in the youth choir, we even sang a song about it, but this was the first time that word came directly to me. I remember feeling excited because God heard me. Let me help you; this isn't one of those "God said wait, I waited, and now I have everything I want" kind of books.

It is 2024, and I. Am. Still. Single. Not only am I still single, but God is still instructing me to WAIT. That's a difference of 17 years, but what's important is HOW I am waiting. I am now waiting IN purpose and ON purpose. Even if God decided not to answer, even if his final answer is no, I have learned that I can be content and move forward with life. It took time to get to this point, but I want to share with you some ideas that have helped me along this journey.

Wait Means Yes

Let me take a beat and give you a little background. I am a mom to a rambunctiously adorable now 7-year-old son, Brayden, and God has used parenting to speak to me in countless ways. What I am about to share with you is the most iconic lesson God has taught me through my parenting relationship. I'm in the kitchen one day washing dishes, and my then 3-year-old walks in, and the conversation goes something like this:

B: Moma, can I have a snack?

M: Wait a minute, let me finish these dishes.

B: (Starts to cry)

M: Calm down, baby, my hands are wet and soapy. Just give me a minute.

B: (Crying still)

M: (still washing dishes) B, I'm trying to get the dishes washed so that I can start dinner. I will gladly give you a snack in just a minute when I finish because, right now, my hands are wet and soapy. Wait just a minute. (yes, I talk to him like a little adult)

B: (FULL ON TANTRUM)

M: (exasperated) Baby, Wait means Yes!

B: (calms down immediately)

Holy Spirit: (nudges) That's what I've been trying to tell you.

It seemed like the more I tried to get him to calm down, the worse the tantrum got. I didn't realize at such a young age that he didn't understand the vocabulary or the reason. If you are reading this book, you definitely understand the vocabulary; you just may not always understand the reason. God has a purpose for everything; we just aren't always privileged to understand His plan or reason.

"Wait" is one of the hardest things we are asked to do, but it's important, and it is one of the most common things we are asked to do. Going to the doctor, you must wait. Calling in to customer service, you must wait. Pampering yourself: hair, nails, makeup, you must wait. Shopping online, you must wait. The reason we struggle with waiting on God is we are missing details. God doesn't tell us how or when the waiting will end. We just have to believe He heard us and wait for His timing. Here are some examples of waiting in which God came through on his promise:

Wait meant yes in **Genesis 15** when the Lord appeared to Abram and promised him descendants like counting the stars in the night sky. Abram was about 75 years old when this covenant was made, while Sarai, his wife, was about 65. Yet Abram and Sarai couldn't see past their physical state to trust God, so they interfered. But God sent reminders in chapters 17 and 18 that they would have a son. That covenant isn't realized until chapter 21, when Sarah gives birth to Isaac. This miracle happened 25 years after the initial promise, but for a woman in the bible days, the wait was much longer than that. Prime childbearing years today are the early 20s, and Sarah was already well past that when the initial promise was given, but God was not concerned with that. Wait means yes.

Wait meant yes in **Exodus 3** when the Lord appeared to Moses and promised to free the children of Israel and lead them to a land following with milk and honey. Yet even after all the miracles they witnessed during their escape from captivity, they still did not have the faith to take the land. The Lord gave Moses instructions in Numbers 13:2: "Send out men to explore the land in Canaan, the land I am GIVING to the Israelites." The scouts went out, explored for 40 days and returned with this report, "We entered the land you sent us to explore, and it is indeed a bountiful country—

a land flowing with milk and honey. Here is the kind of fruit it produces. 28 But the people living there are powerful, and their towns are large and fortified." (Numbers 13:27-28). They got to glimpse what belonged to them, but didn't trust the promise, so they had to wander in the wilderness for 40 years. But when God makes a promise, he can't help but keep it and wait means yes, and the Israelites were victorious over the Canaanites in Numbers 21.

Wait meant yes in **1 Samuel 16:12** when Samuel is instructed to anoint David as king because the Lord had rejected Saul. However, David was not made king for quite some time. He did serve as King Saul's armor bearer and then later as his commander over the men of war. But David became prominent in Israel, and Saul became envious and set out to destroy him. Twice while on the run for his life, David was presented with the opportunity to kill Saul but refrained because he honored Saul as the appointed king. There are about 15 years between David being anointed king and his ascension to the throne. It was quite a wait, especially when you consider all of the obstacles David endured, but we must remember that wait means yes.

As we look at these bible stories, we are reminded that God ALWAYS answers prayer like any good parent answers their child.

Waiting with Purpose

There are benefits to waiting, just as there are dangers to rushing. As I said before, "wait" is the hardest thing we are ever asked to do, but it is the most important. Waiting has 3 purposes: protection, provision, and preparation.

We must remember that God is our father, and He is a good father. When He commands us to wait, His goal is to protect, provide, and prepare. I remember being a new mom, and while I wanted to exclusively breastfeed, that was sadly not my experience. Due to production struggles, I had to supplement to ensure the health and well-being of my son. I remember the first time I had to prepare a bottle for him. My heart hurt because this was not what I had planned, but it was necessary. There were several things I did in that short time that mimicked our heavenly father. In order to protect my son's fragile immune system, I opted to use distilled water versus tap water, which may carry germs. These germs are essentially harmless to me but could be dangerous for a little one. I also had to provide the water and the formula necessary to supplement. This was made difficult because of his sensitivity to cow's milk. It took several tries to find the milk that he could keep down but also that he would actually drink. I would also have to pay close attention to identifying his hunger cues. When I first noticed these cues, I would begin preparing his bottle. I'm an avid researcher, so I learned that if he was crying for a bottle, then I took too long. Preparing his bottle was getting the right water-to-milk ratio and shaking it well so that it was evenly mixed. However, preparing a breast milk bottle was a little different. After pumped milk has set out for a while, the milk fat and the water separate. Before you can feed it to the baby, it has to be mixed up again; however, shaking a breastmilk bottle is not recommended as it can damage the live cells in the milk, lessening the protection. It is better to stir a breastmilk bottle if you want optimal results. So, you must know your gift, and know what you are waiting on. You have to know when to shake and when to stir. It's the difference between being straightforward and subtle. It seems insignificant but can be a major difference in your level of protection.

Protection

This is the part where I talk about "him." The imitation that almost cost me everything had it not been from God's protection. When God has a purpose for your life, the enemy will pull out every trick to cause you to stumble. The most common trick is the counterfeit, the fake. I remember as kids, my sister and I were looking for my mom a gift for Mother's Day. We didn't have much money, but we didn't want the day to go by without honoring her. So, we went to one of the dollar stores and bought some perfume that said, "if you like [insert designer perfume brand here], you'll love our [insert generic name]. Seemed like a great idea at the time, but after my mom used it consistently for several days, we noticed some changes. First being huge whelps all over her body, and she was fatigued almost to the point of being incoherent. After a trip to the emergency room, where her blood pressure was off the charts, we learned that she had a serious allergy to this perfume and that it was wreaking havoc on her skin and blood.

Early part of 2016 (8 years after I first heard the instructions to wait). I was introduced to what I thought I wanted: a hood Christian. He was extremely handsome, with just a little bit of edge, said he loved God, and initially, he presented himself as the man created to love me. Within six months, we were engaged and expecting. Immediately after announcing my pregnancy, his behavior toward me began to change. It was subtle at first, and even though I could feel the discomfort in my relationship, he always blamed my sensitivity on my pregnancy hormones. I fell for that for a while, but soon, I began to seek God, and the rose-colored glasses came off. I could see him for who he really was. I took off my engagement ring and stopped all my wedding plans. I knew I didn't want to marry him but was still holding out hope for him to still want a relationship with our son. A trip to the emergency room alone after I almost fell, which caused some pain in my belly and pelvis squashed that hope. I tried for 10 minutes to wake him up, the man who up until this point woke up every time, I went to the bathroom suddenly couldn't wake up. It was at this point that I knew I had fallen for the counterfeit. One week after having my son, I had to stay with my mom because he was gone, and I needed help because of the c-section. I called him and ended things. It wasn't pretty, and he cursed awhile, then he'd cry, apologize, and then curse some more. I had talked to God, and I knew this was not what I wanted, nor was it what God promised. It was at this point that I began to question

God. I prayed for this relationship. I had asked for signs and wholeheartedly believed that God had spoken and given me the green light. Yet here I was, 33 years old with a newborn and no husband, and now my son doesn't have a father. The guilt and shame of that last sentence was heavy. I was postpartum, and depression was riding me hard. There were times when I'd have some extremely dark thoughts. I was also learning about his infidelity and his financial irresponsibility, which was now being placed squarely at my feet.

Here is the truth: before the Lord saved me, I could be mean and vengeful. If someone hurt me, I was going to find a way to get even. After learning that he was cheating on me since the week after we found out I was pregnant, that he left me in the hospital the night after I had my son to be with her, left me home alone with a 5-day-old to take her out for Valentine's Day, I was feeling really vengeful. I began plotting my revenge, and I knew I would probably get caught, so I was just going to get my revenge and then end my life. In the middle of my scheming, my son woke up crying. My mom tried to console him, but he wouldn't calm down. She handed him to me, and he immediately got quiet. He just wanted me. It was at that moment that I knew why God allowed this baby. He was my saving grace. He kept me grounded to the earth. He saved me from the postpartum depression that wanted to take me out. He saved me from the vengeful thoughts that would have caused me to commit multiple crimes that would have forfeited everything. God's protection in that moment came in the form of a baby born outside of the marriage covenant. God has the aerial picture of our lives, and his wisdom creates protection even when it doesn't feel like protection. Like that of a parent setting guidelines and rules for their children. Protection feels like punishment to the child.

I didn't fully understand this level of protection until six and a half years later. I was watching an episode of "Dear Future Wifey" Podcast with Laterrius R. Whitfield, and in season 5, there was a couple entering divorce. While watching this episode, I felt extremely uncomfortable, but I couldn't explain why until close to the end. She was detailing several instances in which he had purposefully hurt her, starting with an incident on their wedding night, and I watched him sit with zero remorse towards her. He showed no compassion towards the woman he was married to for over ten years. I began to cry uncontrollably. The Holy Spirit whispered to me, this would have been you, trapped in a loveless marriage with no significant friendships. Walking away from this relationship was necessary for my physical, mental, emotional, and spiritual health.

While I was not a baby in Christ during this season of my life, I was not mature enough to have been able to bounce back in Christ. Marrying this counterfeit would have sent me spiraling away from God. I would have blamed God for this pain because I prayed and got what I perceived to be a green light. However, looking back, I realize I was so focused on what I WANTED to see that I was blind to the red flags. Watching this woman pour out her heart, describe how she built him up when he had nothing and see the complete disregard, he had for her sent me into praise. I immediately began to thank God for his protection.

Provision

Provision to God looks different than it does to us. When I asked God for companionship, someone to spend and share my life with and to create our own family, and He said wait (which we know means yes), I just knew the next step was a date...a boyfriend, something along those lines. But the first thing God gave after that prayer and answer was a house. A. Big. Empty. House. Okay, it was moderately sized, but it was EMPTY. I didn't even have enough furniture to put in each room. This felt wrong. I remember distinctly saying to my copastor, Lady Kim Williams, that while I was grateful for the house, it felt like I asked for a PlayStation but got a Wii. Both are amazing gifts, but not what I asked for, and they allow for different functions and games. I didn't have God's vision, and I didn't realize that this gift would be PROVISION for not only me but for my family as well. After getting pregnant with my son and realizing that I didn't want to marry his father, through all of that emotional turmoil and financial struggle, I never had to worry about where we would live. God had already provided a way. I couldn't appreciate the provision in the beginning, but looking back, I give God praise every day that he took care of me when my thoughts were foolish.

God's provision is not situational. God wasn't preparing me for my desire; he was preparing me for life and ministry. My home has allowed me to help several people in my life as they transition through their lives, but it also taught me to be independent. I remember talking to my mom as a teenager, and we had this car that always needed something done to it. We were at a gas station near our house, and she pulled in to pour in some power steering fluid, which had to be refilled frequently due to a leak that we couldn't fix yet. She told me to come watch her so that I would know how to do this on my own if I should ever need to. My comment to her was, "No, thank you, I'll just call Triple A." She laughed because she knew I was so serious. However, owning my home has taught me that it is not always necessary or cost-efficient to always call someone else to fix issues. I have learned to unstop toilets, change locks, assemble toys/furniture and more. I am and always have been a very girlie girl. This was made possible because I could always call on my daddy or my Papa for hard things. My dad passed away in 2011, and my papa two years later. With the major men in my life gone, I quickly found that not many other men would rush to my aid. Asking for help is already a struggle for me, so when I ask, and I'm dismissed or put off, I stop asking and start researching.

Preparation

God provides, God protects, but it is OUR job to prepare. God desires and requires partnership. God works THROUGH us. When I initially heard the command to wait, that was exactly what I did. I just waited. I figured that allowing time to pass would bring me closer to my desire. I continued about life as usual and just expected things to fall in line. I am embarrassed to admit exactly how much time I wasted JUST WAITING. I erroneously assumed that I was ready for what I was asking for. So grateful God knows more than I ever will and did not give me what I thought I wanted then because I would have seriously messed it up. Here's what you need to know when entering a new phase of anything: preparation is necessary.

College is the preparation needed for specific careers. Training is the preparation needed for a job. God gave us dominion over the earth. "Then God said, 'Let us make human beings in our image, to be like us. They will reign over the fish in the sea, the birds in the sky, the livestock, all the wild animals on the earth, and the small animals that scurry along the ground.'" (Genesis 1:26 NLT). This scripture details how we are to have power over other living things, but I believe Psalms

8:6 adds an important element to this power, "You gave them [man] charge of everything you made, putting all things under their authority." In order to get the full concept of this meaning, we have to remember Genesis 1:26, "Let us MAKE human beings…" we are part of the things God made; therefore, he requires us to have dominion over ourselves. The fruit of the spirit are all INDIVIDUAL characteristics that we must possess and demonstrate; "love, joy, peace, patience, kindness, goodness, faithfulness, gentleness, and self-control' (Galatians 5:22-23). Neither of these characteristics can be matured through outside forces. Preparation is our part of the contract.

When we look at the fruit of the spirit, we should be able to identify one (or more) areas that we need to work on. If you are drawn to this book, then I am sure you understand the struggle I have with that "patience" the KJV calls it "longsuffering." The word alone makes my eye twitch, which is a glaring red flag that I still have work to do. We are born in sin, and our sinful nature and the sinful nature of those around us can cause trauma. Oxford Dictionary defines trauma as "a deeply distressing or disturbing experience." As a society, we have added qualifiers as to what can be labeled as trauma or traumatic. It's important to note that while those big ideas of trauma are damaging, there are some small ideas that are just as traumatizing. Absent parents, for whatever reason, can cause distress to several of those Gal.5:22 characteristics. I have spent over 30 years of my life feeling like I have to handle things on my own because of parental trauma. As a child of divorce, my dad, for a period of time, was absent, causing abandonment issues. My mom was battling her own depression and had just enough energy to go to work to provide necessities that she had nothing left for parenting. Hyper independence was what I learned because if my parents, the people who created me and are supposed to love me the most, wouldn't meet those needs, then why would anyone else. I stopped expecting people to show up for me, which led to me not alerting people when things were happening, not celebrating birthdays and having a serious case of anxiety during the planning of my baby shower. Carrying even just this small trauma into a relationship is dangerous and could have catastrophic consequences. So, I need to prepare myself spiritually, emotionally, and physically.

Spiritual Preparation

We must make sure that we are lining up with God's word if we want his abundance. Matthew 5:45 reminds us that God "gives his sunlight to both the evil and the good, and he sends rain on the just and the unjust alike" (NLT). Even when I was in the world doing what I wanted, God still provided, and He still protected. Romans 6:1 asks a vital question, "Well then, should we keep on sinning so that God can show us more and more of his wonderful grace?" (NLT) He's a good father, so he takes care of his children, however, if we want his abundance, we must ensure that we are walking in his will. In order to walk fully in what God has for me, I have to prepare myself to handle those blessings. Spiritual preparation may look like reading spiritual books, including but not limited to the bible, attending a church that teaches the unfiltered word of God, and surrounding yourself with godly people.

I grew up in church. Most Sundays my mom dropped us off at Sunday school and then would come back to enjoy Sunday morning worship with us. My grandparents were assistant pastors of a small family church for as long as I could remember. I grew up loving God, his word and understanding the need to have him in my life. However, it wasn't until college that I recognized the difference between just knowing God and being in a relationship with him. Yet, it wasn't until being home during the quarantine of 2019-2020 that I began to actively work on my spiritual health. I began to seek information on how to live a godly life when everything in society attempts to draw my attention away from God. I began listening to sermons on YouTube and listen to podcasts with some amazing men and women of God, but the most influential addition that helped my spiritual health was developing a prayer life.

"Pray without ceasing" (1 Thessalonians 5:17 KJV). If you have attended 2 or more church services, you have heard this scripture quoted. I knew I needed to talk to God. I would give thanks for life, health, and strength. I would ask for protection and blessings and let him know that I would always give him praise, but during the quarantine, my prayer life shifted. I went from thanking and asking, to worshiping and LISTENING. Prayer is a conversation, and while I may not hear an audible, deep, booming voice of God talking back to me, He does speak.

Emotional Preparation

There is a popular phrase that says, "Hurt people, hurt people." I think this phrase needs to be amended to say, "Hurting people, hurt people." We have all endured hurt at the hands, actions, and words of others, just as our hands, actions, and words have hurt others. However, every person is not walking around intentionally hurting others. Taking the time to heal your heart, whether by seeing a counselor or therapist, getting in God's presence, or reading self-help materials, assists in moving the hurt into the past and allows you to move forward and not transfer that hurt to others. After ending my engagement with my son's father, I took a break from dating, a good long break. There was so much that happened in that relationship that I knew, any man who walked into my life then would not get the best version of me. I was guarded, not just for me but also for my son. I was angry at everyone, me included. I didn't trust anyone, not even myself. I believe it was so fitting that God gave me a son. After this heartbreak and embarrassment, I was so ready to be done with men. I remember joking with my baby sister that I was switching teams. While that was a joke, it came from a real place. I didn't want to be hurt again. My sister, being the straight shooter that she is, let me know that hurt is a possibility in every relationship. Brayden's mere presence wouldn't let me carry hate for the male species. My goal of giving Brayden a childhood that he didn't have to heal from would not allow me to hate what he would grow into: a man. I knew I was going to have to raise him to have healthy self-esteem and self-worth. He was going to need me to speak life into him, especially since I was the only parent around. The biggest step toward emotional healing was a gift from God. I am the spitting image of my father, which was never an issue until my parents divorced. My mom struggled with kindness towards me for a while because I am the spitting image of my daddy, and he really hurt her. So, while my mom and I have discussed this time at length, and we have clarity and peace now, I knew I didn't want to do that to my son, and neither did my mom. The fact that when I look at my son, I see him as the spitting image of my sisters is a gift from God. You'll understand the importance of this later in the chapter "Waiting Room," where I discuss my sisters at length.

However, I believe the way my son loves me has healed more of my heart than any book or counseling session ever could. The moment we revealed to the world I was having a boy, boy moms would always say, "Boys love their moms." It didn't make sense until it did. I chose to co-sleep because it worked better for me at the time. I remember coddling him and singing him to sleep, it was the most natural thing in the world to me. However, I was not prepared for 2-year-old Brayden to roll over in the middle of the night, throw his little leg over me, and make me the little spoon. I laughed about this with my friends, but this display of affection became the norm for him. If we are sitting at the dinner table, he leans on me while he eats. While watching a movie on the couch or in the theater, he slides his hand under the sleeve of my shirt. He'll be playing in his room, and suddenly, without warning, he'll walk into my room and hug me. He is hyper-aware of my presence. I think the moment that I fully understood the "boys love their mom" phrase happened in the summer of 2023. Our library hosts different activities every day to engage kids. They had brought in a magician as a guest. His last trick involved a very, very large balloon. Brayden got up from his front-row seat, walked over to me on the sideline, covered my ears, and then watched the show from the side. This may not seem like much to you, but I am seriously afraid of balloons. I have had panic attacks from them popping. I didn't always feel seen, but my son sees me.

In order to prepare emotionally and start healing, you have to be willing to have hard conversations with a professional, with family and friends, with God or with yourself through journaling. You can even do a combination of all four. Being a single parent made seeking professional counseling difficult, but I did the others as often as possible. I have godly friends who don't let me hide and require me to show up as my best self. I have an extensive digital library that built me back up.

Physical Preparation

Physical change can apply in many ways. You may be looking at your physicality or your physical space. Some of the requests we have for God may require us to make serious physical changes to our bodies, our homes, or our locations. After I had my son, I realized I was not a healthy person. So, I began to make serious changes to my lifestyle in order to prepare to be present for my son long term. I joined Weight Watchers to get a healthier relationship with food. Initially, the goal wasn't to lose weight but to be healthy. I wanted to be able to play with my son. As a single mom of an active kid, my sedentary lifestyle was counterproductive to our relationship. He is such an extrovert, and he craves activity, but my body couldn't keep up. After I watched my son cry silent tears during the pandemic because we couldn't leave the house, I knew that I had to do something so that I could take him to visit places and get active. I addressed my unhealthy addiction to food and my avoidance of physical activity. Even though weight loss wasn't the goal, it was a result of my efforts. The greatest reward came when I took my son to a jump park, and we jumped on trampolines for over an hour, and I didn't pass out. His infectious giggles were all the payment I needed in that moment. It made it all worth it.

As we begin to walk the path God has called us to, we need to be sure we can handle the level of success He is capable of giving. Pastor Mike Todd of Transformation Church said it this way, "God can only bless you to the level your body can take it." This phrase hit me hard because even though it is something I am working on, it is still a struggle. Chips and cookies helped me through my parents' divorce, every breakup and every career failure. I am still learning the discipline for this preparation, and I am still learning to use and lean on the tools I have learned throughout this process. Your body is not the only place of physical preparation.

As God gave me clarity and direction in this writing process, I would share it with my circle of friends. I was facetiming with my cousin Sharetta, excited, because I finally knew what to say about preparation when she asked me, "So how are you preparing?" I gave what I thought was an excellent answer. I detailed the work I was allowing God to do in my heart, how I was reading books and watching podcasts to help heal my brokenness and cope with my emotions. So, she edited her question, "That's all-good work, but how are you preparing your home for your husband?" This excellent and targeted question was met with silence. I was so focused on work within that I hadn't taken the time to look at my physical space. She told me about a mentor of hers who, in her waiting season, bought a trunk and began to put items that she might need as a wife in it: his and hers cups, negligee, cologne for him she liked etc. At this point in our conversation, I was not ready for this high of a leap of faith, but I did take a step. I began cleaning out my closet and drawers so there is space for him whenever he shows up. Think about what you are waiting for. What can you do in the present to physically prepare your heart? Mind? Emotions? Home? It does not have to be huge gestures. Baby steps in your eyes are faith moving mountains in God's eyes. Take a moment and think about what you are waiting for God to do for you, through you and with your life. Use the lines on the next few pages to detail some steps you can take to prepare PHYSICALLY for your dream.

____

____

____

____

____

____

____

____

Wait Time

I am an elementary teacher by trade and skill, and there is a technique we use with students when asking questions. When teaching new content, it is necessary to allow wait time for student response. It is during this time that students are expected to work through their background knowledge and add to it the new content to formulate an appropriate response. I have noticed that there are generally two kinds of students: 1) the one who craves the wait time in order to make the right choice. 2) the one uncomfortable with the wait time and will say anything to avoid the silence, even if the question is not being asked to them. I taught first grade for one year (one year was enough; 1st grade is hard for teachers and students). The majority of the students in that class were uncomfortable with the wait time. Any time I would ask a math question, and they weren't sure about the answer, somebody would ALWAYS yell, "THREE!" This would inevitably lead to rapid guessing. As the teacher, I had to learn not to accept the guess as the correct answer because it is counterproductive to the lesson objective. The lesson objective is directly related to a skill; guessing doesn't activate or strengthen the skill. However, silence to these students feels uncomfortable and causes feelings of inadequacy.

They would say literally anything to pretend to be actively working or thinking. I also noticed that my students took their cue from me. If I looked antsy or annoyed with the wait time, the guessing started sooner. However, when I was calm during the wait time, they actually utilized the time to think critically.

This is where it pays to have godly men and women around you who give good counsel. Right before my breakup, I remember my aunt asking me a question. After visiting with my boyfriend at the time, she looked at me and asked, "You know you've outgrown him, right?" There was silence for a moment, and I was uncomfortable and immediately started asking questions and justifying: "What do you mean? We've been through so much together. He helped me learn to love myself." In other words, I was yelling out THREE! None of that had anything to do with the truth she had just laid on me. I was not ready to hear what she had to say and trampled the wait time. Had I just taken a moment to sit in the wait time, I would have noticed that while we both loved God, I was developing an intimate relationship with God while he was merely an acquaintance. We broke up shortly after this conversation with my aunt, but in my heart, I was still holding out hope that we would reconcile. It took me longer than I'd like to admit to completely walk away.

Submitting to God requires that we get comfortable with being uncomfortable. God makes it clear that "My thoughts are nothing like your thoughts," says the Lord. "And my ways are far beyond anything you could imagine" (Isaiah 55:8 NLT). Armed with this knowledge, we must know that God will not approach situations in the same manner we would. He has the advantage. He's present in not only our conversations and heart posture but conversations and heart postures of those connected to us. As we utilize the wait time and take our background knowledge and add it to the new content God is giving (through His word, the Holy Spirit and discernment), we are able to formulate an appropriate response.

Having godly counsel also gives you a place to focus. When I am uncomfortable, I can look to those who have an intimate relationship with God AND love me to center myself and calm down enough to sit in the wait time. Something I bulldozed through with my aunt. I felt as if I had invested too much time, love and effort to just walk away.

When Wait Feels Like No

Music is an important part of my life; it has gotten me through all stages of my life. Bizzle has a song called "You Don't Know," and one of my favorite lines in this song says, "The reason you don't have it is because God loves you." Oftentimes, we believe that when we don't have what we want, it is some kind of punishment, and that can't be farther from the truth. God will withhold no good thing from us, according to Psalms 84:11, as long as we do what is right.

Waiting is NOT easy, but sometimes it is necessary. However, waiting on God is like waiting for a woman on date night: frustrating and uncertain in the moment, but worth it. There is a story I read to my 1st graders and my son named "Waiting Is not Easy" by Mo Willems. This story is about two best friends, Piggie and an elephant named Gerald. Piggy turns to Gerald and announces he has a surprise for him. Gerald is excited in the beginning, but as time goes on, he gets really impatient. Piggy and Gerald wait all day for the surprise, and Gerald goes through a gamut of emotions from excited to worried to disappointed. Piggy never waivers because he knows that the surprise is indeed on the way, no matter how emotional Gerald gets. Piggy represents God because he changes not; he knows all. He knows the promise is on the way and encourages us to hold on. I relate so well to Gerald in this story because I have also gone through a range of emotions while waiting. When the wait gets long, is when the wait begins to feel like no. Gerald does find out that the surprise was worth the wait.

There will come a time in your waiting process when you WILL question God. I grew up hearing that we should never question God, which made this part of waiting extremely difficult. My genuine concern, hope and curiosity felt like a sin. When my personal relationship with God and my parenting style collided, I realized the flaw in this line of thinking. If you have spent any amount of time with kids, you are aware that they ask A LOT of questions. A study in 2018 determined that kids 4 and under ask, on average, 73 questions a day within a 14-hour time span. While this is tiring, it is acceptable because we are aware that our littles are new here and they are learning about the world around them. So good parents do the best they can to answer as many questions as possible, even if it means turning to Google or Siri. As a parent, not only am I accommodating when my son asks me questions, but I have also been known to encourage it. Our relationship with God is a parent-child relationship. Matthew 7:11:

"So if you sinful people know how to give good gifts to your children, how much more will your heavenly Father give good gifts to those who ask him." If, in my sinfulness, I can have compassion for my child's natural curiosity, then it stands to reason that he will show that same compassion towards me; after all, I am made in his image. Being new to anything requires asking questions, which includes Christianity and all that goes with it. The God of the universe is not phased or offended by your questions.

In the beginning, my questions stemmed from curiosity, and they covered vast topics from frivolous to serious purpose. What does he look like? Does he like thick chicks? Will he want to live in the city, or does he enjoy this small-town feel? Will he support my career and my ministry? However, as the wait extended, the questions shifted. Did God really say wait? Is he listening to me? Did my current mistakes cause him to change his mind? Wait was starting to feel like no. At this point in my waiting, I began to get angry, and I stopped hoping. Yet, everywhere I went, God sent people to remind me to wait, to encourage me to wait and to keep hoping. Transparent moment: at one point in this season, I stopped even presenting myself as desirable. I'd show up to places without putting effort into how I looked beyond being clean. That is saying something from the girl who, as a teen, wouldn't walk to the dumpster without a face full of makeup. If I'm being honest, even now, there are days, weeks, months even when wait feels like no. This is when faith becomes critical to the journey. At the height of the pandemic, I decided to use that time to work on myself. So, I began watching podcasts and reading books.

While watching an episode of The Basement with Tim Ross and guest Jackie Hill Perry. Ross said something that came alive for me. Ross says, "Faith is HOPE, not certainty. Trust requires empirical data; faith is different. Faith says I don't know what you can do or what you will do. It's simply hope." It was at this moment that I realized I was using the words faith and trust interchangeably, yet the requirements are different. Faith is the beginning, and it grows into trust. Faith is when I don't have a reference for what I am asking for, but I am hoping for it. Trust is built after prolonged exposure. For example, I was working for a nonprofit organization, my mom held down two steady jobs, and my middle-baby sister was in college. My mom was suddenly down to one job, and it wasn't enough to cover all of her necessities, especially with a child in college. I was consistently attending a bible study group with other young adults. I had just started consistently paying my tithes, and the first time my mom needed some assistance, I was faced with the dilemma of helping or paying tithes. At that moment, I felt led to do both. Looking at numbers, I knew I couldn't do both, but I took a leap of faith. This scenario was new, and I wasn't sure how it was going to work out. Between the 3 of us, we each had our own apartments and cars. Making the choice to do both was nothing but faith. I got to see God show up for all three of us with limited income for 6 months or more until we could consolidate back to one home. Those months of consistent exposure to God's provision, God's multiplication turned my expectation from faith to trust. I have witnessed his provision repeatedly, so I trust he is going to show up like he always has. This started as faith, but it grew into trust. This is an important lesson to learn. You can trust God in one area of your life but struggle to have even mustard seed faith in another. I am the perfect example. I wholeheartedly trust God to meet my physical needs, and he has shown up consistently in that area. I confidently walk around singing the song "I don't know how/God's gonna do it. I don't know when, when He's gonna fix it. I only know, God's gonna make a way for me. I know he's gonna do it, VICTORY!" However, there are still days when waiting for my kingdom spouse feels like no, and I wonder if He's going to fulfill his promise of companionship for me.

In the chapter, Wait means Yes, I detailed three stories in the bible where God instructed his people to wait and how God provided for them. Yet, for us, it is just a few chapters that separate the promise from the manifestation. However, it was 20 years before Abraham and Sarah embraced Isaac. It was in this period that Sarah, began to rationalize and scheme to help God. I can almost hear her thoughts. Well, God made that promise to Abraham, not me. He promised that HIS seed would be numerous, not mine. When our thoughts deviate from what God promised, the enemy steps in. It's in this season that we attempt to help God, but usually, this just causes more trouble and complications. Sarah's attempt to help consisted of her giving her servant to Abraham (without Hagar's consent, I might add), and the birth of Ishmael. Jealousy took up residence in Sarah's heart, and she began to mistreat Hagar to the point where Hagar ran away. When Sarah becomes pregnant with Issac, she has Abraham send Hagar and Ishmael away so that Isaac doesn't have to share his inheritance. Sarah's attempt to help God was anything but helpful. We must learn from Sarah. When the wait begins to feel like no, we need to remember to keep our hands out of it. When I was a kid growing up, the adults in my life would say things like, "Stay in a child's place and out of grown people's business." Well, we are all God's children, so I say to you, "Stay in a child's place and out of God's business."

Respect the No

Let me get the hard part over with early. God tells us no sometimes. He is our Father, and any good earthly father tells his children no to things, situations, circumstances, and places that have a high potential to be detrimental to their physical, mental, emotional, or spiritual health. I remember hearing a sermon where the speaker said, "God's promises are yes and not yet." But this particular lesson omitted God's no. My niece is a recent two-year-old, and no is hard for her to hear. When we say no to her about anything, instant meltdown. However, we say no to things and activities that will bring her pain and/or discomfort. No, you can't put the coins in your mouth. No, you can't climb on the wobbly chair to get a random cup that doesn't belong to you. No, you can't play with the toy that has five hundred seventy-three little pieces to it. As an adult, you can clearly see the dangers in all those situations because you have experience in those areas, whether personal or learned. My niece does not. She is unable to see the big picture. She doesn't see the danger in potentially swallowing a coin or the general germiness of it all. She doesn't recognize that the chair is unstable, her balance is unstable, and the cup may belong to some random person in which it is not a good idea to share drinks. However, our family recognizes those things and does the best we can to prevent adding unnecessary pain or discomfort to her life. God, our Father, recognizes things in our surroundings that might cause us unnecessary pain or discomfort, and His goal is to eliminate that risk.

As the mom of an exceptionally intelligent boy, saying no is difficult sometimes. He doesn't always understand why I say no. He is so unbelievably logical that he can make an argument for his way of thinking easily. The problem lies in his immaturity granted he's 7, but that lack of real-world experience influences that logic. Because he has a limited worldview, his logic is not always, well, logical. He assumes that if something bad happens, he will have enough time to make adjustments so that he isn't negatively affected. However, as his mom and the adult who supervises his care, I am well aware that unfortunate things can happen in the blink of an eye. It's in these moments when either I struggle to explain my no or he struggles to understand my no; I say this simple phrase. "Respect my no."

I first heard this phrase when scrolling on TikTok. Influencer and author Destini Ann Davis introduced this phrase as a way to end negotiation for rules that are nonnegotiable. This phrase reminds him that while he may not understand the reasons for my no, he does need to respect it. I am usually not a "because I said so" mom. I have no trouble explaining to my son my thought process for the choices I make concerning him. I believe that talking through my thought process helps fine-tune his own thought process. I am trying to teach him how to think and how to think for himself. So I will model that for him. However, there have been times when I could not accurately articulate my thought process, or I thought my process was beyond what he could comprehend at his age, and I elected to limit my explanation. We seem to think that because the world sees us and labels us as adults, God does, too; well, let me tell you, he does not. You are still HIS child. At my big age, if I called my mom and told her I didn't feel good, she'd immediately spring into action to get me what I needed: medicine, peace, food, etc. If I tell her that someone on my job upset me, she is ready to march down to my place of employment and talk to my supervisor on my behalf or a coworker or whoever the culprit may be. Because no matter how grown I am, no matter how many bills I pay, I am still her baby. You are still God's baby and just like I determine that my son isn't ready for all the details of every choice that I make. God makes that same determination concerning us.

At the homegoing service of a dear friend, the man of God said, "God doesn't owe us an explanation." We have to operate from the understanding that God is good. If I truly believe that God is good, then every choice he makes, every path he directs me on, is going to benefit me. "For the Lord God is our sun and our shield. He gives us grace and glory. The Lord will withhold no good thing from those who do what is right." (Psalms 84:11 NLT). When God says no, evaluate the situation. The word just told us that God wouldn't withhold good things from us, so if he's saying no, then it might be because the thing we are asking for isn't good or we aren't doing what is right.

I don't want you to get distracted when I say maybe our request isn't good. God is in the details. Whatever the request, God will ensure Proverbs 10:22, "The blessing of the Lord makes a person rich, and he adds no sorrow with it" (NLT). So, while the request itself may be good, if the details or the path is not, we must respect God's no. There is nothing wrong with desiring a successful business, but if you look at the wrong partner, respect God's no. Wanting to increase your family is good, but if you are struggling financially, respect God's no. Desiring to get married is good, but if your current partner is not being led by God, respect God's no. No is for your protection. We call God our

Father but override his fatherly love, advice and decision-making. Let him be the father in your life.

The other option for no is if we aren't walking in the path necessary. If we aren't doing what is right, then God may withhold good things. Proverbs 10:22 makes a promise, but it requires something from us. We must walk in obedience to God in order to receive his blessings. At a homegoing service in 2012, a friend I hadn't seen or talked to in over 5 years hugged me and then prophesied. She gave some direct eye contact and said, "God said, write the book." At this instruction, I didn't have a frame of reference for what it could possibly be about, so I dismissed the idea. It was radio silence for several years after that, and I forgot the commandment. However, in 2021, several different people would say to me, in private, "God said write the book." In February of 2021, Prophetess Jasmine Bartley spoke at a women's conference at our church and after service, she also said, "God said write the book." At this point, everything changed. My heart was open to be obedient. Once again, this was spoken directly to me, not openly over the mic. When I got home, I knew exactly what to write about, and in less than a month, I had a working title and about 6 chapters outlined in the notes section of my phone. I began typing out the book and creating an outline. In 2022, things changed yet again. In the first part of the year, I was intentional about creating time to write, however, as the year progressed, I became really relaxed in the writing process. God would still speak to me concerning the book, and I would make notes on my phone, but I stopped making time to cultivate and enrich what he had given. I overheard my best friend teaching her son, and it convicted me. She told him, "Delayed obedience is still disobedience." Even though I was still kind of doing what I was supposed to do, it was not in the time that God required. So, since I did not do my part concerning the promise, God could not do his part.

The Deception of Contentment

One of my favorite bible stories is the story of Hannah in 1 Samuel chapter 1. Most people like to discuss the rivalry between Hannah and Peninnah. But that's not what sticks out to me. Hannah is married to Elkanah. You all know the story of how Hannah had no children, but Peninnah, the other wife, had children. While Peninnah had Elkanah's children, Hannah had his heart. 1 Samuel 1:3-5 talks about how every year they would go to Shiloh to worship, and while there, Elkanah would offer sacrifice. He would then give portions of that sacrifice to Peninnah and her children, but verse 5 says, "But to Hannah he gave a double portion because he loved her, and the Lord had closed her womb" (NKJV). Yet her desire was STILL to have a son. Her desire was great and Peninnah would provoke her to the point she would get so emotional about it that she wouldn't even be able to enjoy the celebration.

It's important to note that having children was the main way a woman could bring honor to her family. This was especially true for having sons since sons would stay with family and would add their wives and children. Also, since women had minimal rights, having a son would ensure a woman's well-being in the event her husband died. Hannah wanted honor and security. However, her husband tried to force her into contentment. When she'd get upset and refuse to eat, verse 8 "Then Elkanah her husband said to her, "Hannah, why do you cry and why do you not eat? Why are you so sad and discontent? Am I not better to you than ten sons?" People in your life will attempt to push you to the extreme version of contentment. The version in which you accept whatever is handed to you, with no desire for more. Content simply means to be satisfied. It's important to know that you can be satisfied with where you are, with what you have, and still desire more. You can appreciate the apartment and desire the house. You can appreciate the Honda while you desire the Tesla. You can appreciate the husband and desire the kids. You can appreciate the meal and desire the dessert. It does not have to be one or the other. The deception of contentment attempts to make us choose one thing or another. That is a trap and NOT what God wants for us. Don't believe me? I got proof: "Take delight in the Lord and He will give you the desires of your heart." Psalms 34:7. Hannah had the love of a good man, but that did not stop her desire for a son. Hannah did not fall into the deception of contentment. She went to the temple and prayed. She was so distraught that Eli, the priest, thought she was drunk. (1 Sam 1:10-16). "11 And she made a vow saying, 'Lord Almighty. If you will only look on your servant's misery and remember me, and not forget your servant but give her a son, then I will give him to the Lord for all the days of his life, and no razor will ever be used on his head." This prayer blesses me because as Hannah prayed, according to verse 13, no sound left her lips. Eli initially thought she was drunk, but once he realized how fervently she was praying, he agreed with her in prayer. Without even knowing what the request was, "17 Eli answered, 'Go in peace, and may the God of Israel grant you what you have asked of him.'"

Hannah prayed in her heart and made a vow in her heart, and even though the prayer was soundless, God understood her request. Hannah had a husband who loved her fiercely. She still asked for the son. God answered her prayer. They went back home, and in due time, Hannah became pregnant and gave birth to a son, Samuel. It's important to remember the vow Hannah made to give him back to the Lord. She kept him with her until he was weaned, and then she kept that vow. She took Samuel to Eli and reminded him of who she was and let it be known, I prayed for this child. Eli didn't know what she was asking for, yet he agreed with her anyway. I don't know what your request is from God, but I agree with it anyway. That could be the end of the story, and we could thank and bless him right there, but I feel like those sales commercials when the guy says, "But wait…. there's more." Because there is indeed more.

Hannah asked for ONE son, but Eli in 1 Sam. 2:20 blessed the couple and asked God to grant them other children. Hannah was content with ONE son, but our God is a God of abundance. "Now to him who is able to do immeasurably more than all we ask or imagine, according to his power that is at work within us," Eli asked, and God delivered. Hannah, after being barren, gave birth to four sons (including Samuel) and two daughters (Ephesians 3:20, NLT). This is the part that really got to me. Hannah got exactly what she asked for: a son. She honored her vow, and the man of God asked to give her more. Reminds me of Brayden. No matter what adventures we go on, he is always looking forward to the next thing. He enjoys the moment, but he is always planning for the next. At breakfast, he will enjoy the oatmeal but is already asking about his lunch and a snack. While buying a toy in Walmart, he is so excited that he opens it in the car, but as soon as we get home, he reminds me of the toy we didn't get and makes plans to go back to Walmart tomorrow to get it. He has enjoyed watching Sonic 2 at the theater and even at home, but he is already creating the cast for Sonic 3. He told me we needed to find someone really famous to play Shadow. This got me thinking could this be why in Matthew 19:14, "Jesus said, 'Let the children come to me. Don't stop them! For the Kingdom of Heaven belongs to those who are like these children?'" Little children have vast imaginations, and they are not bound by the realities of this world. When asking their parents, grandparents, aunts/uncles for things, they just keep asking. They don't fall into the deception of contentment. Children are always EXPECTING! They expect basic needs, they expect their wants, they expect their dreams; as parents/family members, we attend to those needs, wants, and dreams. We must remember what Matthew 18:3-5 says:

And he said: "Truly I tell you, unless you change and become like little children, you will never enter the kingdom of heaven. Therefore, whoever takes the lowly position of this child is the greatest in the kingdom of heaven. And whoever welcomes one such child in my name welcomes me." (NIV)

We get to call God father and that comes with bonuses. As parents, we are attuned to our children's needs. However, the older they get, we allow them the space to ask for what they want/need. We wait for them to realize that they need our help. The same is true for our Heavenly Father. He is attuned to our needs and desires, yet he has given us the space to ask for them. Don't fall into the deception of contentment, thinking you can't ask for peace because you asked for hope yesterday. Don't think that you can't ask for mended relationships because you asked for healing last week. Be like little children and allow your imagination to run wild and free because whatever you can imagine, God can do abundantly more.

Don't Just Do Something, Stand There

Whenever an emergency arises in our life, we want and expect a resolution to happen quickly, efficiently, and effectively. We are in such a rush that sometimes, we ignore the signs. The word *something* is vague. Oxford defines *something* as a thing that is unspecified or unknown, which could literally mean anything. Whatever is going on in your life is too important for such vague terminology. Your dreams, goals and desires are far too important to just do something. "My thoughts are nothing like your thoughts,' says the Lord. 'And my ways are far beyond anything you could imagine. For just as the heavens are higher than the earth, so my ways are higher than your ways and my thoughts higher than your thoughts" (Isaiah 55:8-9). Our thoughts are so far from God's thoughts that the way we think about resolutions could be considered ungodly. We are limited to logic, and God has the benefit of being sovereign, so what he says is law, even if it defies our logic.

Transparency moment: I am a procrastinator, especially when it relates to anything social. I am a natural introvert; my social battery drains rapidly and requires quiet, alone time and/or worship to recharge. So, grocery shopping is one of my least favorite adulting tasks. I will put off going to the grocery store until we have 1 egg, a corner of milk, the ends of the bread, and a scoop of butter left. In Small Town, Texas, the choices of grocery stores are limited, but either way, I'd choose H-E-B. The customer service is top-notch, the produce is amazing, and pricing is always within budget. The trouble is, a lot of people in my small town feel the same way, and H-E-B is ALWAYS packed. The crowded store always drains my social battery and drains it quickly because while HEB customer service is great, the people of HEB, not so much. My shopping experience always starts out good, but sooner rather than later, that social battery begins to drain, and I begin to rush to get out of the store and away from the crowd. It is always in this situation that I will inevitably forget something important to everyday life in my family, which results in me having to return to the store. (Insert facepalm here). I worked with a teacher who would often say to her students, "If you don't have time to do it right, you must have time to do it over." I have had to learn how to navigate the grocery store in these times such as creating a list. I've also had to learn not to wait until the utter end of our groceries before going to the store. I know that when I make that mistake, we need more items than my social battery allows.

The same can be said about our spiritual walk with God. Sometimes, we are in such a rush to get to what God has for us or the instructions he has given that we leave out or forget important ingredients or tasks. Sometimes, it's not WHAT we forget, but WHO we forget. If you need a biblical reference, take Saul, the first King of Israel. Samuel, God's fulfilled promise to Hannah, was to meet Saul, God's answer to Israel, in order to prepare to fight the Philistines again. The relationship between the Israelites and Philistines is a toxic one. The Philistines had been an enemy of the Israelites for ages. God would grant Israel victory over the Philistines, but they would soon forget Him and begin worshiping idols. The Philistines would show up and enslave the Israelites. Then the Israelites would cry out to God, and he would show up and deliver them again. In one of these tense moments, Saul divides the army; 3,000 go on with him, and he sends the rest home. A little while later, the 3,000 is divided again. 1,000 goes to Gibeah in the land of Benjamin with his son, Jonathon, and the other 2,000 follow Saul into Micmash. Jonathon attacked and defeated the Philistines at Geba, starting that toxic cycle all over again. The Philistines gathered "as many warriors as the grains of sand on the seashore!" (1 Sam. 13:5 NLT). At this sight, the men of Israel began to hide, and some even escaped. Saul and his men were afraid. They were waiting on Samuel as instructed, but saw the immediate danger and the fear gripping his troops. In verse 9, Saul demanded, "Bring me the burnt offering and the peace offerings!" And Saul sacrificed the burnt offering himself." As soon as he finished, Samuel arrived. Saul's impatience and disobedience come with some serious consequences. "'How foolish!' Samuel exclaimed. 'You have not kept the command the Lord your God gave you. Had you kept it, the Lord would have established your kingdom over Israel forever. But now your kingdom must end, for the Lord has sought out a man after his own heart. The Lord has already appointed him to be the leader of his people because you have not kept the Lord's command.'" (1 Samuel 13:13-14). Impatience is expensive. Saul's impatience led to disobedience, and it cost him EVERYTHING! What will you lose by rushing into action? God's timing is perfect because he has the best view concerning you. But his actions didn't just affect him but also his lineage. When God rejected Saul as king, he also rejected his sons and grandsons as future kings. What has your disobedience cost your family?

Waiting Room

Now is the time to evaluate Who is in the waiting room with you? The people you surround yourself with can enhance or hinder this waiting season. The people in the waiting room with you should be an extension of your faith. So, when you are struggling to believe, struggling to even hope, they can stand in the gap and remind you what God said: pray with you and for you. Let's talk about some important people who need to be in the waiting room.

I remember when I went to the hospital to have my son. This was pre-pandemic, so visitation wasn't rigid. However, there were still some rules to follow. My sisters and ex-fiancé were present most of the day. However, if and when anyone else showed up, they would have to sit in the waiting room until one of those 3 came out. Everyone I know wasn't invited to his birth. The same should be true about the birth of God's promise to you. Everyone can't be privileged to witness this miracle. Be careful who you invite into this space. You need people who will encourage and support you, especially when labor intensifies. I have been blessed to have some amazing women in my life. These I am about to talk about right now hold an extremely special place in my heart because of the work they did in the waiting room with me. My sisters, Toya and Brea, my cousin Sharetta, and my bestie, Rainy, play an astronomically large role in this part of my story. These women refused to let me give up in the wait. They would speak encouraging words to me and send TikToks and podcast clips reminding me that God always comes through on his promise. They would pray for and with me whenever I asked and even when I didn't ask. They would hear God and then be willing to share what He said with me, even though they knew I was struggling to believe in his promises. They believed FOR me until I could stand on my own and believe for myself. They would listen to me when I was super excited and hyped in my belief, and they listened in those moments when I was down and couldn't bear to hope anymore for fear that I was forgotten.

Sharetta's memory is unmatched. She would remind me of specifics God had sent directly to me concerning this promise. I remember feeling so defeated on the phone with Sharetta once, and she brought up the very first dream God gave me. I was so deep in my doubt and disbelief that I couldn't remember the dream. However, she remembered almost every detail. She remembered that we met outside at a park and that he had the most beautiful brown eyes. She remembered that this dream was like a highlight reel of dates for us, ending with us in front of an arch exchanging vows. She remembered so much of it that I could see it again as she talked; I can see it now as I am typing. She wouldn't let me forget. You need people in your waiting room who will REMIND you of your worth, value and the promises of God.

Rainy is a prayer warrior that does not play with the enemy concerning those she loves; she is also gifted to interpret dreams. She interpreted a dream about a love interest who couldn't accept my boundaries. The boundary crossed in the dream was so small it seemed harmless. However, I listened to her enough to take a step back and truly listen to what he was saying and within the week, he clearly showed me that he didn't plan to honor my boundary concerning intimacy. I had spent a substantial amount of time in prayer breaking soul ties and had I not had her in my corner, I could have ended up in the same struggle again. Rainy later allowed herself to be really vulnerable with me in obedience to God. Our single season has some similarities as we were both single moms to young boys. She called me frantic about a conversation. It was about a dream she had concerning me and my future spouse in an argument. God impressed upon her to share some tips and wisdom with me. Lessons she'd learned with her husband. While still in the waiting, she wanted to ensure I was equipped with the knowledge necessary to make wise decisions. She sent me a voice memo at 5 in the morning after the birth of her twins, and she was still in tears from her prayer, a prayer FOR me. This mom of TWINS under a year old woke up at 5 AM to pray for ME! You need people in your waiting room who will go to the throne on your behalf. Lazarus was sick unto death, but his sisters went to God on his behalf. I thank God for the prayers of my best friend.

Brea is the jokester of this group. I can usually count on her to make me laugh when life gets rough. She is also an encourager. She compliments me often about my parenting, my teaching, and yes, even about the physical. I have been single for 7 years now, and I mean single single. Brea is the one who video-chats me and notices I've done something different with my hair or that I've tried a new lipstick shade. This is a phenomenon because Brea couldn't care less about hair or makeup. The closest she comes to owning or using makeup is ChapStick, and she went from locs to a fade. Yet she ALWAYS notices and comments. She called me one day in a really serious tone, which is unusual. During her quiet time with God, He began to talk to her about me. She said, "Sis, God hasn't forgotten. It's closer than you think." What she didn't know was that before she called, I was praying. I was telling God I felt he had forgotten about me and His promise. God didn't wait until Sunday morning to respond to me, He sent my sister IMMEDIATELY. Not just any sister, but the sporadic churchgoer sister. He chose an unlikely vessel, but one that I would hear because it's unusual. Brea is a lot like our father. She may be the youngest, but she often takes on the role of protector, both of my siblings do. This past year, I have spent focusing on myself, growing my relationship with God, healing and becoming the best version of me I can be. I've been watching online sermons and podcasts, conversing with my mentors and leaders, and reading books about healing and spiritual growth. Brea and I share a love of books. So, when she asked me to send her my book wish list, I didn't think twice because I figured she was looking for some ideas. Immediately she sent me a Barnes and Noble gift card to purchase a book or two to read during the summer. This was the decoy while she plotted to purchase ALL of the books on my list, which she accomplished just in time for my birthday. When she messaged me to check my email, she said, "Somebody's got to spoil you until Mr. God Sent comes." I like gifts like the next girl, but it was the gift of bettering myself that warms my heart the most. You need some people in your waiting room who will help you grow and encourage you along the way.

Toya is the world's BEST Hype (wo)man. I wish I could see myself through the eyes of my middle-baby sister. She has no doubt that I can do whatever she asks. She trusts that if I can't do it, I'll just talk to God, and He'll do it for ME so I can do it for HER. This belief is wordlessly beautiful to me because Toya has seen me at my lowest points in life: after every breakup, after every failure, after every mistake (real or perceived), she still encourages me. She can find the silver lining in every flaw. She has learned to give me a moment to feel, but she refuses to let me wallow in any negative emotion. This balance is important. She is wise enough to recognize that my feelings and emotions are valid and they need an outlet. I can vent to her and unload to her and she is present through this process. She gets to hear my passive-aggressive comments, the ruthless comments brought on by the frustration of the situation. This expression is necessary because I feel heard. Oftentimes, when Christians are wronged, the community immediately pushes the forgiveness narrative. Don't misunderstand; forgiveness is necessary, but it should NOT be the immediate focus. Toya allows me to have my human emotions and feelings and she validates them. Feelings are not right or wrong; they just are. You need people in your waiting room who understand that and will allow you to experience and express those feelings, even the negative ones. The mark of a true friend is that they don't allow you to set up residence in your feelings. This is that balance: feel, but don't reside. When my son's father and I split, she allowed me to cry, and she brought me cookies and candy since alcohol wasn't an option. Yet, she also showed up (and STILL shows up) for me and my son. She drove us to postpartum appointments, cleaned my cesarean wound after I ripped my stitches, and drove me to see a lactation consultant an hour away so that I could continue to breastfeed. She allowed me to feel the pain of a failed engagement, a failed co-parenting relationship, and a failed friendship, but she didn't allow me to stay there and sulk over my negative feelings. You need someone who sees you, the good, the bad and the ugly, but still shows up for you and pushes you toward greatness. Paul and Silas were in jail together, but they didn't let the other one fall into a depressive state. Toya and Brea are the Paul and Silas in my life, and they constantly and consistently encourage me.

Friends not only push you toward the best version of you, they also call out the negativity. We often assume that when people call out our flaws, they are hating. I picked up my son from school, and he had gotten into trouble at school for telling another little boy, "I'm not your friend anymore." When I talked to him in detail at home, I learned that my son had cheated during the recess game of freeze tag, and this friend told on him. It was at this point that I had to teach my son that REAL friends, let you know when you are wrong. I asked him if cheating was the right thing to do and if he wanted to be known as a cheater. He answered no to both questions. I reminded him that my friends let me know when my thinking is flawed.

The people in my waiting room don't just encourage me, they correct me as well. When I broke it off with my ex-fiancé, he decided he wasn't going to be present in my son's life. I mentioned to Sharetta that I might as well just tell Brayden his dad died since he wasn't going to be involved. Sharetta immediately shut down that thinking. She told me that not only would I be lying to my son but that if and when he learned the truth, he could potentially blame me for their lack of relationship. She also had me consider the ramifications of him potentially mourning twice. Once from my lie and second from discovery and then realizing that his dad didn't want to be involved. She would not allow me to risk tainting my relationship with my son due to my hurt from his father. Due to this, I have had to face some seriously hard questions about his father, but any time I am unsure how to answer, I can always depend on Sharetta to pray with me and talk me into a kid-appropriate answer: one that is NOT dripping with disdain for the man that abandoned the person I love the most on this earth.

If you are not part of a church community or you are not involved in your church community, I would highly encourage you to do both. My leaders, Pastor Myron and Lady Kimbrely Williams are the starting place of the blessings. These beautiful humans speak directly to me on a weekly basis. They don't just speak of blessings and prosperity. They also correct and rebuke, but they do so in love. I had to submit myself to their leadership. When the counterfeit came, Lady Kim tried talking to me, but I was too "in love" to hear her. So, she just started praying. On Sunday mornings, her hugs were a little longer and I knew she was praying even if she never told me she was praying. The love they showed to me during this rebellious season is truly a reflection of God's love for us. They encouraged me to continue to participate in service. I truly believe their prayers sent God's protection. Here's the grace in all of this: neither of them, after the fallout, came to me and made me feel anything less than loved and a daughter of their ministry. As I entered into single motherhood, they would show up randomly with essential baby items. I'd be using the last pack of wipes and Lady Kim would stop by and drop off some wipes or some onesies. Once my six weeks were up and we were allowed to attend services again, I showed up worried. How was I going to provide for this baby alone? This wasn't part of my plan. I never said anything, but Pastor Williams finished his sermon and then turned and began to minister straight to me. God spoke directly to me through him, and everything he said, God backed up. My pastors embraced me the same way Elizabeth embraced Mary when she showed up pregnant and unmarried.

None of the people in my waiting room would allow me to forfeit God's promise to me. Their prayers, encouragement, and correction were like Aaron and Hur in Exodus. The children of Israel were enslaved by the Egyptians. In the midst of their slavery, God sent Moses back to Egypt and made promises to them. "Therefore, say to the people of Israel: 'I am the Lord. I will free you from your oppression and will rescue you from your slavery in Egypt. I will redeem you with a powerful arm and great acts of judgment. I will claim you as my own people, and I will be your God. Then you will know that I am the Lord your God who has freed you from your oppression in Egypt. I will bring you into the land I swore to give to Abraham, Isaac, and Jacob. I will give it to you as your very own possession. I am the Lord!'" (Exodus 6:6-8 NLT) Yet the Israelites were so discouraged that they couldn't even believe the promises. Yet, God still gave Moses instructions to fulfill His promise. And he did just what He promised. Pharoh put the Israelites out of Egypt. As they traveled to the promised land, God protected them, not allowing them to travel the main road that passed through Philistine territory. The wilderness was not only God's plan, but it was his protection. While on the way to their promise, they were attacked by Amalekites. "Moses commanded Joshua, 'Choose some men to go out and fight the army of Amalek for us. Tomorrow, I will stand at the top of the hill, holding the staff of God in my hand'" (Exodus 17:9 NLT). Joshua followed instructions, while Moses, Aaron and Hur went to a hill. Moses held the staff over the battle, and the Israelites maintained the advantage, but when he dropped his hands, they lost it. Arron and Hur sat him on a stone and held his arms to ensure the Israelites victory over the Amalekites (Exodus 17:10-13). When my negative thoughts seemed to have the advantage, the people in my waiting room held up my arms to maintain my advantage. You need some people in your life whole will stand with you in battle.

www.ingramcontent.com/pod-product-compliance
Lightning Source LLC
Chambersburg PA
CBHW050015040726
47599CB00014B/1391